Shooting the STORY

Shooting the
STORY

Outstanding photojournalism from Montreal's La Presse and The Gazette

The Gazette

Photographs:

Front Cover: **Dave Sidaway, David Bier, John Kenney, Pierre McCann, Bernard Brault**
Back cover and end papers: **Gordon Beck**
Cover flaps: **Bernard Brault, Peter Martin**

Canadian Cataloguing in Publication Data

Main entry under title:
    Shooting the Story
    Issued also in French under title: Chasseurs d'images
    ISBN 1-895600-16-2

1.   Montreal Region (Quebec) – History – 20th century – Pictorial works.
2.   Quebec (Province) – History – 20th century – Pictorial works.
3.   Photojournalism – Quebec (Province) – Montreal.
I   Robinson, Jennifer
II.   Jasmin, Yves
III.   Gazette (Montreal, Quebec) IV. La Presse (Montreal, Quebec)

TR820.C422 2000   779'.9971427   C00-901030-0

Editor: **Jennifer Robinson**
Associate Editor: **Yves Jasmin**
Design: **Luna Design**

ISBN: 1-895600-16-2

Legal deposit, 2000
National Library of Canada
Bibliothèque nationale du Québec
Printed in Canada

Published by:

The Gazette
250 St. Antoine St. West
Montreal, Quebec
H2Y 3R7

and

La Presse
7 St. Jacques St.
Montreal, Quebec
H2Y 1K9

A rainbow of colour on this hot air balloon silhouettes its owner at the Festival des Montgolfières in Saint-Jean-sur-Richelieu.

Photo: **Dave Sidaway**

In perfect form, this Doberman clears a hurdle at a Montreal dog show under a sign that spells WOOF.

Photo: **Marcos Townsend**

Montrealers caught in the Bonaventure Depot floods of 1886 pose for George Charles Arless, one of the city's foremost photographers of the day and the first of four generations to capture Montreal on film. George Charles learned his trade at the Notman Studio, where he worked for nine years before opening his own studio in 1875. His grandson, Richard (Buster) Arless, was one of The Gazette's first staff photographers, joining the paper in 1938. Great-grandson Richard Arless Jr. is still shooting pictures for The Gazette.

Foreword

What makes a great newspaper photograph? Most photographers would say "it's just f8 and being there" – being in the right place at the right time with a loaded camera. But anyone who has ever tried his or her hand at photography knows it's not that simple. Much more goes into taking the great photos that light up the pages of your morning newspaper. It takes a photographer's artistic eye and instinct, intuition and a sense of humour, sensitivity and insight, the ability to anticipate a crucial moment in the action, an understanding of the story and of the human condition and, sometimes, raw courage.

Shooting the Story is a collection of 200 outstanding photographs that celebrate the talent and work of the photographers at Montreal's oldest French and English newspapers, La Presse and The Gazette. They are outstanding because they capture unique and fleeting moments, gone in the blink of an eye. The composition is so complete that they tell their own stories. Some of the photos will make you smile or laugh. Some are simple moments of everyday life that have their own sense of history and importance – a police officer feeling for a pulse on a homeless man, a family in mourning, a group of elderly men playing checkers in a park, the miracle of giving birth. Still other photos recall tragic events, disaster and loss that have made headlines. All too often, the front pages of newspapers, like history, reflect violence and conflict rather than beauty.

We did not set out to publish a book that documents historically significant news events or celebrities. Instead, we wanted to pay tribute to the photographers who report the news in pictures and to showcase the quality of the photojournalism that appears daily in the news pages. Our photographers were asked to submit some of the best work of their careers. The photos were selected from among the hundreds submitted and from among the millions of images in the archives of the two newspapers, based on the quality of photojournalism irrespective of how important the news event was. In selecting the photos, we tried to strike a balance between bad-news photos and good, between disaster and humour, between the front-page tragedies and the pleasant things in life that often don't make big headlines. It was a difficult choice. Photographers for La Presse and The Gazette have taken many more great pictures during their careers than we could possibly include in a book this size.

Henri Cartier-Bresson, one of the most influential photojournalists of the twentieth century, wrote that the best photographs capture "the decisive moment" – a unique moment in which the elements and composition of the photograph are so perfect that it tells a universal story, with little explanation needed. These are some of the best photographic stories from the pages of The Gazette and La Presse.

La Presse photographers Rodolphe Carrière (left) and Lucien Desjardins steady their Graflex cameras for a shot. La Presse ran this photograph of the newspaper's two staff photographers on Oct. 13, 1934, as part of its 50th anniversary celebrations and wrote: "Always on the road, each time with a different reporter, their job is important; there is no one from the top of the social hierarchy to the bottom that they have not viewed through their camera. With journalistic initiative and ability, they report the news in pictures." The pencil outline and cut-out background was a commonly used method of highlighting subjects in photographs for better reproduction in the pages of the newspaper.

In the early days of newspaper photography, cameras were clumsy and the few pictures that were published tended to be fuzzy and posed. One of the most widely used cameras was the Graflex, a clunky box held at waist level. The photographer viewed the image by looking down, as shown in the 1934 photo on the previous page.

By the 1940s, photography had become a serious tool for reporting the news. Technological advances had made it easier to shoot news photographs and to reproduce the images in the pages of newspapers. By then, the Graflex had been replaced as the camera of choice by the more versatile Speed Graphic, which was held at eye level. The photographer viewed the subject through a viewfinder attached to the top of the camera. Still, by today's standards, the Speed Graphic was clumsy and slow. For each photo, the photographer had to change the film holder, replace the flashbulb, sight and focus the picture, set the proper lens aperture, cock the shutter and then click the shutter release button to take the picture.

Photographers had to anticipate the perfect shot and if they missed the moment, they had to crank up their cameras again and hope for another chance. It was with a Speed Graphic that Roger St-Jean of La Presse shot the wonderful photo on page 107 of Maurice Richard hugging Elmer Lach. St-Jean had intended to shoot the winning goal but, distracted for a moment by an usher, he had missed the moment. Instead, he shot the wonderful scene after the goal and captured a moment no one else had.

The use of 35-mm film cameras became common in the 1950s and 1960s. But it wasn't until the 1980s that colour film was regularly used and that The Gazette and La Presse regularly published colour photos on the front page. With advances in printing technology, the use of colour is increasing throughout the paper. Today, cameras have motor drives capable of shooting eight frames per second. Faster film makes it possible to capture dramatic images in lower light, without a flash. Faster shutter speeds freeze action in crystal clarity in thousandths of a second. Long lenses mean that sports photographers don't have to wait for the action to come to them; they can zoom in on the action. Today, more and more, newspaper photographers are using digital cameras that need no film and that transmit images digitally over phone lines to their newspaper computers and to newspapers around the world – all this in a split second. André Pichette's photo on page 141 of a woman kissing the hand of Premier Lucien Bouchard at a Parti Québécois meeting is an example of a digital image.

Jennifer Robinson / Editor

Acknowledgements

Many talented people participated in the production of this book. Special thanks to publishers Michael Goldbloom of The Gazette and Guy Crevier of La Presse for their inspiration and support. Guy Granger, La Presse's assistant managing editor, and Alison Marks, The Gazette's manager, New Products, were central in making the book a reality. My counterpart at La Presse, Yves Jasmin, who was responsible for the French version of the book, Chasseurs d'images, was a source of inspiration and support. His experience and attention to detail were invaluable. The advice and guidance of veteran photo editors Jean Goupil of La Presse and Barry Gray of The Gazette were much appreciated when it came time to make the difficult decisions about which photos should appear in the book. Many thanks to Roland Forget of La Presse and Patricia Desjardins of The Gazette for their enthusiasm in tracking down many of the prints and negatives.

So many great newspaper photographs have been lost or misplaced over the years. It is only recently that newspapers have begun to recognize fully the tremendous historical significance and value of their photo archives. Thanks to Russ Peden and Edie Austin of The Gazette for lending their copy-editing and proofreading skills to the project and to Wayne Lowrie of The Gazette for his cutline suggestions. Many thanks also to Armand Favreau, Dennis Dubinsky and Arden Lanthier of The Gazette. Finally, without the talent, dedication and hard work of the photographers whose photos are included in this book, Shooting the Story would not have been possible. Newspaper photographers are a special breed, combining a toughness of spirit with an artistic eye, sensitivity and the best of human qualities. Their work offers insight into our lifestyles, lives and history. To the photographers, much appreciation and admiration.

– J. R.

Firemen douse a gasoline tanker after it caught fire in a spectacular accident in Sainte-Madeleine in September 1983.

Photo: **Robert Mailloux**

Flash

Some photographs stand out because they tell stories instantly –
good news or bad. They capture moments in which
the composition and mood are so flawless that they are universally
understood. Some are simple vignettes of everyday life – delightful scenes that
bring a smile or evoke emotions shared by us all. Others are stories of
unthinkable violence or loss. The miracle of birth, a caring hand, a funny
scene at a horse show, the face of grief, courage or death – these are images
that existed only for a split-second and would have been lost
had it not been for the photographer's eye.

On Dec. 6, 1989, a lone gunman went on a killing rampage at the École Polytechnique of the Université de Montréal. He singled out women, killing 14 and wounding 13 other people before shooting himself dead. This photo shows a young victim slumped over a chair in the cafeteria while a man pulls down Christmas decorations. Photographer Allen McInnis got the photo by scaling a wall with the help of some students and shooting through a window. The Gazette decided to run it on Page One after a debate that pitted the news value of the picture against concern for the victims' families. The photo won a National Newspaper Award, Canada's most esteemed photojournalism award, in the spot news photo category.

Photo: **Allen McInnis**

The excitement and anticipation of Haitians waiting in Port-au-Prince for the return of Jean-Bertrand Aristide in 1994 is captured in this striking photo. They were among many who showed up at the presidential palace to cheer Aristide upon his return to Haiti, which was made possible by a U.S.-led military force that restored him to power three years after he had been ousted by a Haitian military coup.

Photo: **Allen McInnis**

A makeshift bus makes its way through the streets of Hargeisa in northern Somalia in December 1991. Civil war, still raging in the south at that time, had subsided in the north. The city's infrastructure had been destroyed by fighting, people were struggling to put their lives back together and 300,000 land mines were still buried in the city when John Mahoney took this photo.

Photo: **John Mahoney**

Tedd Church found himself in the middle of a field, "up to my knees in manure and surrounded by cows and electric fences" after he was let off by the hot air balloon on the right. The U.S. entry was named after Phileas Fogg of the Jules Verne classic Around the World in 80 Days.

Photo: **Tedd Church**

The Americans were pulling out of Vietnam when Bob Carroll of United Press International called Tedd Church to say that this offbeat photo he had sent on the photo network had been published on page one of Stars and Stripes. The U.S. military newspaper had hoped the photo would bring smiles to the faces of retreating forces. Tedd Church's picture, taken at the Montreal dog show, was also published in several magazines around the world and won Church his first National Newspaper Award for feature photography in 1975.

Photo: **Tedd Church**

What started out as a "run-of-the-mill" assignment at Macdonald College for Pierre Obendrauf resulted in this beautifully composed scene of two exchange students saying farewell after a summer of friendship in Canada. Charlotte Peters of Belgium leans out the bus window for a teary last goodbye to friend Bryndis Thorarinsdottir of Iceland.

Photo: **Pierre Obendrauf**

A coal porter hauls his load through the streets of Port-au-Prince to eke out a living delivering coal to poor neighbourhoods. When Allen McInnis was assigned to cover the return of Haitian President Jean-Bertrand Aristide in 1994, he was struck by scenes of poverty like this one. This man earned $5 a day and paid $2 a day to rent the buggy.

Photo: **Allen McInnis**

The funeral procession for René Lévesque, who died in 1987, winds gracefully through the streets of Old Quebec not far from the apartment on rue d'Auteuil where he lived while he was premier from 1976 to 1985.

Photo: **Richard Arless Jr.**

Thousands of people filed by the open coffin to say their last farewells to former Quebec premier René Lévesque in 1987. Lévesque's body lay in state in Montreal and then in Quebec City, where he was buried. The composition of this dramatic shot captures the sadness many felt when this remarkable politician died.

Photo: **Armand Trottier**

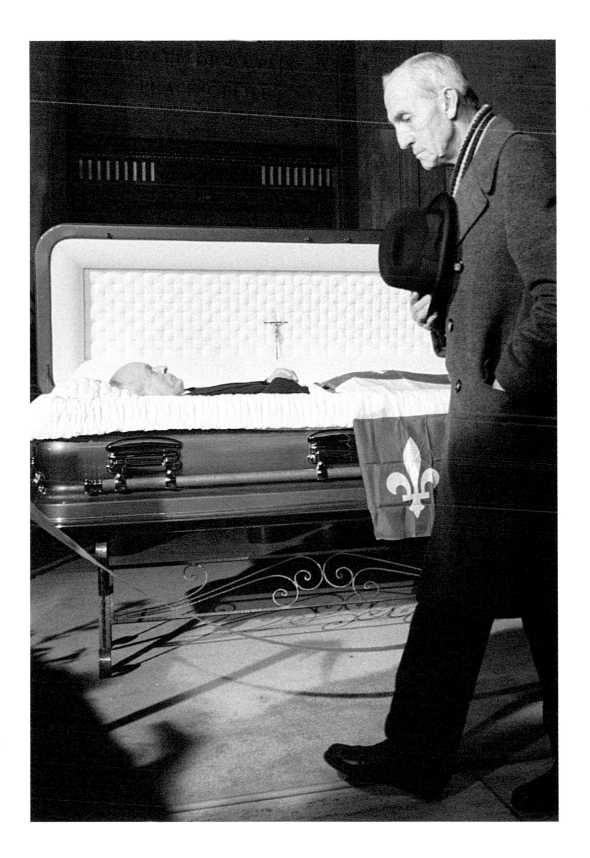

It could happen to anyone. This little girl was so excited to see a flock of pigeons that she didn't even notice she was losing her undies as she ran toward them. The pigeons didn't stick around, but fortunately her dad was there to put things back together.

Photo: **Tedd Church**

A man with a sack and spade walks in Mount Royal cemetery at apple blossom time.

Photo: **Gordon Beck**

The face of courage is captured by this photo of a fireman who had just saved a cat from a burning house on Notre Dame St. in 1969.

Photo: **Michel Gravel**

Terry Fox, shown here on a wet highway during his marathon of hope, had his dream of running across Canada cut short near Thunder Bay, Ont., in September 1980 when he learned that cancer had spread to his lungs. He died the following June, but his courage earned him a permanent place in Canadians' hearts as a symbol of determination and hope. This photo won a National Newspaper Award in 1980 in the Feature Photo category.

Photo: **Peter Martin**

Two nuns peer out their window to check on water rushing from a broken main on St. Antoine St. in December 1967.

Photo: **Michel Gravel**

When you've got to go. . . . A loyal mount waits for its young rider outside a johnny-on-the-spot at the annual horse show in Foster in the Eastern Townships. Tedd Church, photographer-on-the-spot, won the 1981 National Newspaper Award for feature photography for this delightful scene.

Photo: **Tedd Church**

A pair of joggers round a bend on Beaver Lake on a calm misty morning at 7 a.m. and Tedd Church was ready with his camera to capture the scene. The colours, composition and mood convey the serenity of the moment.

Photo: **Tedd Church**

A Montreal policeman checks for a pulse on a homeless man lying on a bench in Lafontaine Park in east-central Montreal.

Photo: **Gordon Beck**

The ability to spot a funny picture is a talent all good photographers must have when they are sent out on a feature assignment. Pierre Obendrauf shot this simple, yet amusing photo of two nuns shopping for religious ornaments during a gift show at Place Bonaventure in 1991.

Photo: **Pierre Obendrauf**

Many photos of Pope John Paul II were taken during his momentous visit to Canada in 1984 but few capture his compassion and love for others as does this photo taken during his stopover in Montreal.

Photo: **Pierre McCann**

Up, up, and away.
Photo: **John Kenney**

Moonlight on the crest of a ski hill at Mont St. Sauveur at 3 a.m. in March 1993 gives a surreal lustre to moguls below.

Photo: **Bernard Brault**

A young Jacques Villeneuve looks up to his mother Joan during the funeral for his father Gilles in Berthierville in May 1982. In the foreground, beside the coffin of the race-car legend, is Jacques' sister Mélanie. Gilles died in a racing crash. Like his father before him, Jacques has become an idol of Quebec race-car fans.

Photo: **Pierre Obendrauf**

By age 27, Monica Proietti, also known as Machine Gun Molly, had robbed more than 20 banks, netting more than $100,000. Her luck ran out in September 1967, after she and two thugs heisted a little more than $3,000 from a caisse populaire in Montreal North. After a car chase that ended when she crashed into a city bus, she was killed in a shootout with police at the corner of Dickens St., now Villeray St., and Pie IX Blvd.

Photo: **Paul-Henri Talbot**

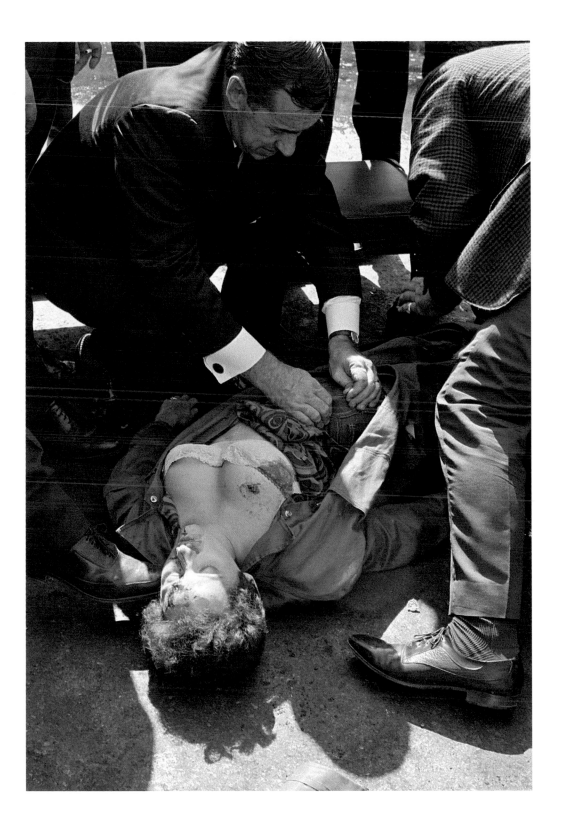

A warehouse in the port of Montreal is taken down.

Photo: **Pierre Côté**

Pierre Elliott Trudeau, his ex-wife Margaret, and their sons Justin and Sasha leave St. Viateur Church in Outremont after a private memorial service for Michel Trudeau, 23, who died in a skiing accident in 1998 in western Canada. The photo captures the pain etched on the faces of a beloved Canadian first family.

Photo: **John Mahoney**

Ramadan, the Islamic month of fasting, was not quite over when Tedd Church took this delightful photo of a young boy, slightly out of step with his elders at prayer time.

Photo: **Tedd Church**

Boys in ballet need a certain strength of character.

Photo: **Marie-France Coallier**

Quebec Premier René Lévesque, his signature Wallabies on his feet and cigarette in hand, tries to make it over a puddle without getting wet. He came up short. Lévesque had been at the inauguration of a park in Longueuil in July 1979 and was in too much of a hurry to leave to walk around the puddle.

Photo: **John Mahoney**

As is the custom every June 24, Quebec sovereignists put their politics on parade to celebrate Quebec's Fête Nationale, also known as St. Jean Baptiste Day. This photo was taken in 1995, four months before Quebec's second referendum on sovereignty.

Photo: **John Kenney**

A Montreal street light, beautifully freeze-framed, sparkles with ice during the January 1998 ice storm. It was one of many that went out during the storm, which destroyed power lines across southern Quebec, eastern Ontario and the northeastern United States and damaged entire forests.

Photo: **Dave Sidaway**

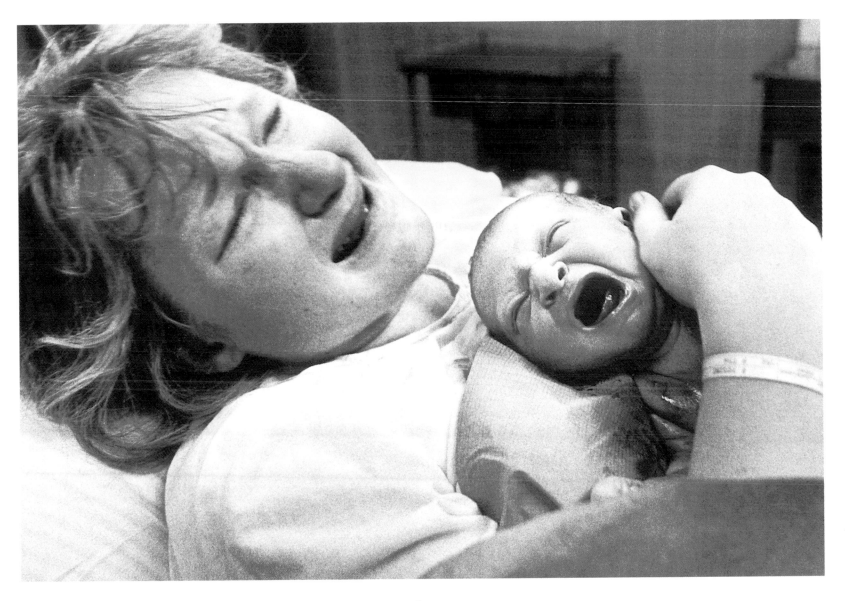

A look of joy and exhaustion on the faces of mother Jocelyne and her newborn son Darryl, seconds after his birth in February 1982, was captured in this photo by John Mahoney, the proud father. Labour had lasted 23 hours. The composition of the photo is simple, yet it conveys the beauty and emotion of the event.

Photo: **John Mahoney**

In 1987, Anthony Griffin, an unarmed 19-year-old man, was shot dead by a Montreal policeman. With this photograph of three family members at the funeral at St. Simon's Anglican church in Laval's Chomedey district, Allen McInnis captured the sense of shock and grief that gripped the community.

Photo: **Allen McInnis**

Reine Johnson gives her son Daniel a motherly touch of pride minutes after he was sworn in as Quebec premier in January 1994. He followed in the footsteps of her husband Daniel and other son, Pierre Marc, who also served as premier.

Photo: **Jean Goupil**

Prime Minister Pierre Trudeau chats with a dancer in costume at a backstage party after a ballet performance in the 1970s at Place des Arts. Tedd Church, who said Trudeau was "chatting up" everyone in tights that night, captured this unusual shot.

Photo: **Tedd Church**

Thousands of federalists swarmed Place du Canada a few days before the 1995 Quebec referendum to show their support for a united Canada. This was one of the lasting images of the campaign. In the referendum, Quebecers narrowly voted against separation.

Photo: **Gordon Beck**

This man took his life by jumping from an apartment balcony, striking at least two balcony rails before hitting the ground. A police officer had tried for an hour to talk him off the ledge, to no avail. Tedd Church shot several frames of this disturbing scene but stopped when the man hit the ground. As a matter of policy, most mainstream newspapers do not cover individual suicides.

Photo: **Tedd Church**

The body of this boy was found hanging on a barbed wire fence in the Gaza Strip in the Middle East in the late 1960s during the Israeli occupation of the area. The boy appeared to be about 12 years old. Tedd Church was spending several days in the area reporting on the conflict when he happened upon this scene. It was not clear how the boy had died.

Photo: **Tedd Church**

Picking up the pieces. A man tries to eke out a living in what is left of his restaurant in 1999 in the old quarter of Pec in western Kosovo. The town had been hard hit by Serb forces. In one part of town, only 17 of 1,070 homes were left standing.

Photo: **Gordon Beck**

While in Armenia in 1993, the photographer was struck by this image of love and hope in the midst of devastation.

Photo: **John Kenney**

Forty-nine people died in Chapais in northern Quebec at a New Year's celebration in 1980 when a man set fire to a Christmas garland during a party in a hall. The horror and senseless nature of the tragedy are captured in this photo of a man looking through body bags to locate the bag containing the remains of the victim whose relatives (standing at the back of the room) had come to identify.

Photo: **Tedd Church**

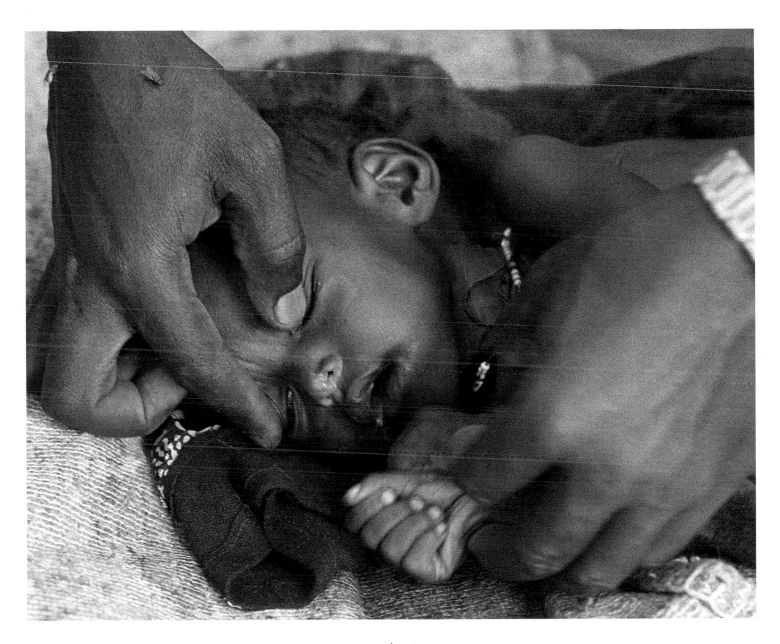

A nurse closes the eyes of a tiny child who had just died in a refugee camp in Ethiopia in December 1991. The baby was one of the thousands of people who died in the famine caused by drought and civil war in neighbouring Somalia. What John Mahoney saw there, while traveling with the Canadian military, still haunts him. This baby was alive in a woman's arms, then started, took a deep breath and died. The woman laid the baby on the ground, and walked away without a word. This photo was nominated in 1992 for a National Newspaper Award.

Photo: **John Mahoney**

Struggle

News, like history, is written in blood and conflict more frequently than in
beauty. To get close to where news is breaking, photographers are often
thrust into situations where they come face to face
with conflict and danger. Sometimes, their own safety is at risk,
whether they are covering a flood, fire or a demonstration that turns violent.
These are some of the images of struggle that have appeared
in La Presse and The Gazette.

Verdun firemen help an injured colleague
after a section of roof fell on two firefighters
battling a blaze at an abandoned Verdun theatre
in October 1997.

Photo: **Allen McInnis**

A helicopter surveys a May 1990 fire burning out of control for three days at Quebec's largest used-tire dump, in Saint-Amable. The fire caused an ecological disaster as black fumes billowed into the air and oily toxins seeped into the ground, contaminating water reservoirs and wells for miles around.

Photo: **Paul-Henri Talbot**

A fireman battles flames engulfing a minivan. Phil Carpenter was en route to an assignment when he spotted a van on fire on the side of the highway. No police or firemen had arrived and the driver was pacing frantically, all alone by the side of the road. Carpenter was the first person to stop and immediately started shooting the blaze, trying at the same time to calm the driver. It was a cold winter day so he lent her his coat and his cell phone until police and firemen arrived.

Photo: **Phil Carpenter**

Protesters try to push over a truck outside Montreal's main postal station as police push back during a violent demonstration in December 1968.

Photo: **Michel Gravel**

Emergency workers, assisted by sea cadets, struggle to save a child pulled out of a LaSalle building that collapsed in an explosion in March 1965.

Photo: **Michel Gravel**

Two unidentified men kick and beat a man on the ground during a 1969 riot in which rival groups clashed in the streets of St. Léonard over language-of-education restrictions.

Photo: **Pierre McCann**

Pierre Vallières, chief ideologue of the Front de Libération du Québec (FLQ), resists arrest at a demonstration in July 1965. Vallières wrote White Niggers of America while in prison, where he spent four years after being convicted of manslaughter in the death of a 64-year-old woman killed in the bombing of a strikebound shoe factory, La Grenade, in 1966. Released in 1970, Vallières later became committed to social causes, gay rights and non-violence. In 1990, he told The Gazette, "I've come to recognize that violence leads nowhere."

Photo: **Michel Gravel**

In January 1998, five days of freezing rain, up to 100 millimetres, fell in some parts of eastern Canada and the northeastern United States. About 2 million homes – 1.4 million Hydro-Québec customers in Quebec alone – were plunged into darkness for up to a month in the dead of winter. In this photo, members of a Rougemont family carry a few belongings out of their home. They had been icebound and without electricity since the start of the storm four days earlier and, when this photo was taken, were leaving to seek refuge elsewhere. The triangle of darkness, the name given to the area east of Montreal in which they lived, was blacked out for 33 days.

Photo: **Denis Courville**

More than 3,000 kilometres of Hydro-Québec's power network broke down during the January 1998 ice storm. In all, 24,000 poles, 4,000 transformers and 1,000 steel pylons, including these shown here, were damaged or destroyed. It was indisputably the ice storm of the century.

Photo: **Armand Trottier**

Residents of Saint-Jean-Vianney salvage what they can after their homes were destroyed in one of Canada's most bizarre natural disasters. On May 4, 1971, a rainstorm opened a 213-metre-wide crater in the ground that swallowed 36 homes, several cars and a bus. Thirty-one people were killed and the remaining 1,500 villagers had to leave their homes.

Photo: **Pierre McCann**

The carcasses of 10,000 caribou line the shores of the Caniapiscau River in northern Quebec. The animals drowned trying to cross the swollen river during their annual migration in 1984. A section of the river was later renamed after former premier René Lévesque in 1997 as part of the Parti Québécois government's 20th anniversary celebration of Quebec's language law, Bill 101.

Photo: **Robert Nadon**

On July 14, 1987, a torrential rainstorm brought Montreal to a standstill, inundating the métro system and flooding the Décarie Expressway with water up to 3.5 metres deep. The deluge dumped 55 mm (2.2 inches) in less than four hours. Motorists abandoned their cars on the Décarie Expressway as flood levels rose and they found themselves trapped. One man died in a flooded underpass.

Photo: **Robert Mailloux**

A firefighter helps a child up a ladder to escape the flooded Décarie Expressway.

Photo: **Pierre Obendrauf**

Water crashes through the streets of Chicoutimi after heavy rainfall and mismanagement of water levels in dams in the Saguenay-Lac-Saint-Jean area led to devastating floods in 1996. In all, 10 people were killed, 12,000 people were forced from their homes and hundreds of homes and businesses were destroyed or damaged.

Photo: **Pierre McCann**

A stairway leading nowhere (above) is all that's left of a house wiped out by flooding that destroyed entire neighbourhoods in Chicoutimi (right) and other towns in the area.

Photos: **Pierre McCann**

Firefighters help tenants escape a burning building that housed Labelle's Bar-B-Q, a Chinese restaurant on Wellington St. in Verdun. This dramatic shot captures the fear felt by the people on the ladder.

Photo: **Tedd Church**

The face of an exhausted firefighter is seen through the icicles hanging from his helmet.

Photo: **Pierre McCann**

A burst of flames knocks over this Park Ave. merchant in October 1992 after he set a city of Montreal flag on fire. The merchant wanted to burn the flag to protest against reserved bus lanes along Park Ave. but when it wouldn't light, he soaked it with gasoline to help things along. Allen McInnis kept shooting when the flag burst into flames beside him. Neither man was seriously hurt.

Photo: **Allen McInnis**

Firefighters battle a blaze in September 1997 that destroyed an art gallery and warehouse on a block west of Old Montreal bounded by King, Queen, Wellington and William Sts. The fire cut power to 8,000 customers in the lower city, including the Gazette building on St. Antoine St. Because of the blackout, The Gazette was unable to process Dave Sidaway's photos before the paper went to press and this photo was never published.

Photo: **Dave Sidaway**

Too little, too late. Firefighters try to pump water from a frozen river to douse the flames that destroyed this house in Saint-Philippe-de-Laprairie in December 1968.

Photo: **Michel Gravel**

District fire chief John Scallion worked for 20 minutes trying to breathe life into a victim of a fire in 1972 at the Canadian Liquid Air building on Sherbrooke St. Photographer Tedd Church had crawled up four storeys in the dark, smoldering remains of the building to reach the rescue site. Church's flash wouldn't work because of the humidity so a flashlight, held by a fireman, was the only light source for this photo. The man was one of five who died in the fire.

Photo: **Tedd Church**

A firefighter battles fireballs on Dec. 30, 1999, after two freight trains, one carrying petroleum, collided in an industrial park near Mont-Saint-Hilaire. The train's engineer and conductor were killed in the crash and more than 500 people living near the tracks had to leave their homes until the flames were brought under control.

Photo: **John Kenney**

A horrified firefighter stands in front of Farina Rahman, the distraught mother of two young boys who perished in a Dollard des Ormeaux fire in April 1992. The brothers were playing with a friend in a bedroom when the fire started. The three boys died huddled together near a window.

Photo: **Richard Arless Jr.**

The driver of this truck thought he could get around traffic stalled on the highway between Montreal and Quebec City by cutting across the ice on the Richelieu River in March 1995. The ice gave way under the weight of the truck and the cargo, carcasses of cows, bobbed to the surface. The driver of the truck escaped unharmed.

Photo: **Pascale Simard**

It's remembered as the Blue Bird Café fire. In fact, the 37 people who died on Sept. 1, 1972, were in a nightspot above the Blue Bird, in a country and western bar called the Wagon Wheel at 1171 Union Ave. Three men, angry because they had been denied admission to the over-crowded bar, poured gasoline on a stairwell floor and set it on fire. People stampeded to get out but the fire exits were locked. All but two of the victims were under 30. The youngest, Eva Towers, was 14. Fifty-seven people were injured. Jean Goupil still remembers his horror and feeling of helplessness as he shot emergency workers removing the bodies.

Photo: **Jean Goupil**

A SWAT team officer points his gun
at a suspect arrested in a bust on
Bagg St.

Photo: **Allen McInnis**

On July 11, 1990, Sûreté du Québec Corporal Marcel Lemay was shot dead during a police attempt to dismantle a Mohawk barricade erected on a road near Oka to prevent the expansion of a golf course. The incident sparked a 78-day standoff, in which Mohawks held out against provincial police and Canadian soldiers. Lemay's killer was never identified. This photo shows a Mohawk warrior, his gun raised in victory, standing on an overturned police car.

Photo: **John Kenney**

John Kenney was working as a freelance photographer when The Gazette sent him to Oka early on July 11, 1990, to cover trouble that had erupted at a Mohawk barricade. Kenney spent the next 11 days caught behind Mohawk lines, covering the story as tension mounted. This photo shows an armed warrior ordering him to stop taking pictures. That summer and fall, Kenney spent more than 40 days behind Mohawk lines as police and soldiers pressed in, smuggling his film past authorities with the help of Gazette reporters.

Photo: **John Kenney**

A soldier pushes Waneek Horn-Miller and a child during one of the many clashes between Mohawks and the military during the Oka crisis in July 1990.

Photo: **John Kenney**

A soldier confronts a Mohawk warrior, an image that captures the essence of the standoff at Oka.

Photo: **Pierre Côté**

A Sûreté du Québec officer clubs a protester during one of the many violent clashes in the hot summer of 1990 during the crisis. This photo was shot August 12 during a clash between police and people who took over a seaway lift bridge in Beauharnois to protest against Mohawks who had closed the Mercier Bridge.

Photo: **Allen McInnis**

Angry men at the LaSalle end of the Mercier Bridge on August 18, 1990, stone a convoy of Mohawks fleeing Kahnawake during the crisis that summer. The Sûreté du Québec had authorized the convoy but when the stoning began, stood back and did little to stop the violence. Pierre Obendrauf's shot was chosen Canadian Press photo of the month.

Photo: **Pierre Obendrauf**

Soldiers are silhouetted against a September
evening sky as the 1990 Oka standoff drags on.

Photo: **Philippe Bossé**

Games

There's more to sports photography than clicking the shutter. The ability to anticipate plays and spectacular crashes, and to capture the emotion and intensity of the game is key to great sports photos. Some of the photos in this section record important sports moments, like the photos of Donovan Bailey and Victor Davis celebrating their victories. Others are special because they capture the emotion of the game – the intensity, disappointment, conflict, anger, aggression, enjoyment – emotions that make powerful photos no matter how important the game. One of the most striking is David Bier's mat-level shot of boxer Rocky Graziano in the ring. Bier was a talented freelancer who set a high standard for sports photography and photojournalism in the 1940s and 1950s in Montreal. Some of his best-known photos were of hockey superstar Maurice Richard.

Bruny Surin flashes a winning smile as he hugs Donovan
Bailey, Robert Esmie and Glenroy Gilbert after their
victory in the 4·x·100 metre relay in Atlanta in 1996.

Photo: **Bernard Brault**

This arm-breaking lift ended the career of Scottish weightlifter John McEwan at the 1994 Commonwealth Games in Victoria. He was trying for a lift of 135 kilograms – which would have been a personal best in competition – when he got into trouble.

Photo: **Bernard Brault**

A Montreal Impact player jumps for joy after the winning goal in a 1994 match.

Photo: **Bernard Brault**

The thrill of victory and the agony of defeat are contrasted in this photo shot after a race.

Photo: **Robert Skinner**

Split-second camera action captured Quebec's freestyle skiing star, Jean-Luc Brassard, flying high to a gold medal at the 1994 Lillehammer winter Olympics.

Photo: **Bernard Brault**

High-flying skateboarder shows his stuff with a jump at a rock music and skateboarding festival on Île Ste. Hélène in 1999.

Photo: **Bernard Brault**

Tiger Woods keeps his eye on the ball as he blasts out of a sand trap at the Royal Montreal Golf Club during the 1997 Canadian Open. The prestigious Royal Montreal is the only course where Woods, so far during his professional career, has missed the cut on the PGA Tour. The composition of this perfectly timed shot – the ball, flying sand and the intensity on Woods' face – is what makes it so special.

Photo: **John Mahoney**

Water polo players huddle before a game, creating
the unusual composition caught by Dave Sidaway's lens.

Photo: **Dave Sidaway**

The elated expression says it all. Dave Sidaway had his camera trained on this soccer player to catch his reaction after he made a penalty kick.

Photo: **Dave Sidaway**

Alexander Wurz's Benetton flies over Jarno Trulli's Prost Peugeot in a spectacular crash in June 1998 at the Canadian Grand Prix in Montreal. Miraculously, no one was injured and Wurz went on to finish in fourth place in his spare car.

Photo: **André Pichette**

First- and second-place finishers were on a roll as they crossed the finish line in the 1992 Montreal marathon. First place in the 12.5 km wheelchair event went to André Viger.

Photo: **Bernard Brault**

They're No. 1. Ste. Anne's rugby team captain
Brad Belvedere is hoisted after the team won
Quebec's Rugby Division 1 championship
game over Ormstown 13-12.

Photo: **Richard Arless Jr.**

Expos catcher Gary Carter, down and out, throws his bat in disappointment after striking out during a game against the Philadelphia Phillies.

Photo: **Robert Nadon**

American gymnast Jennifer Sey cries out
in pain after falling from the uneven bars
at a world gymnastics championship
in what was formerly the Vélodrome.
Her leg was broken, as the pain on her
face suggests.

Photo: **John Mahoney**

The intensity of Maurice (Rocket) Richard's fire-on-ice style is captured in this photo of him beating a goaltender.

Photo: **Roger St-Jean**

Canadiens superstar Maurice (Rocket) Richard and Elmer
Lach jump into each other's arms after the Rocket scored
in a game against the Boston Bruins in the 1950s. Roger
St-Jean, who was shooting the game with a Speed Graphic,
was distracted by an usher and missed the actual goal.
But he made up for it with this famous photograph.

Photo: **Roger St-Jean**

Maurice Richard shakes hands with goalie Sugar Jim Henry after one of the most dramatic goals of the Rocket's career. Richard suffered a concussion earlier in the game but came back, bloodied and groggy, to score the winning goal in the seventh game of the 1952 Stanley Cup semi-finals.

Photo: **Roger St-Jean**

Ushers try to restrain a fan at the Montreal Forum who was angry at the suspension of Canadiens superstar Maurice (Rocket) Richard in 1955. National Hockey League president Clarence Campbell (clutching his hat) had suspended Richard because of an ugly stick-swinging incident in an earlier game, depriving the star of the chance at a scoring title. Rioting broke out during the game March 17, 1955, when this photo was taken, and spread to downtown streets, where rioters smashed windows and clashed with police. Roger St-Jean stood his ground in the kerfuffle to record this moment in Canadian hockey history.

Photo: **Roger St-Jean**

This topsy-turvy waterboard action was caught near the Montreal Casino.

Photo: **Martin Chamberland**

Robert Charbonneau of the Lac-Saint-Louis region looks over at Jean Petit-Frère representing the Bourassa region as they sail over a hurdle during the 300-metre race at the Quebec Games in August 1997. Petit-Frère won the race in 37.83 seconds.

Photo: **Robert Skinner**

The best action is sometimes on the sidelines, as shown by this photo of university basketball players leaping in victory at the end of the McGill Invitational Tournament.

Photo: **John Mahoney**

Victor Davis celebrates his win at a national short-course swimming event in Winnipeg. There's a saying in sports photography that "jubilation often beats action" and knowing how to anticipate the athletes' emotions is the key to great pictures like this one. Instead of shooting the winner at the finish line, Dave Sidaway positioned himself where Davis would see his time after the race finished.

Photo: **Dave Sidaway**

Long Island Rough Riders goalie Manuel Carou takes a hands-on approach to suggest that Darren Tilley of the Montreal Impact not venture too close to him in the crease during a playoff game at the Claude Robillard Centre in Montreal in September 1997.

Photo: **John Kenney**

Athletes come in all shapes and sizes, as this photo of a softball pitcher in Whitehorse, Yukon, shows. Tedd Church shot this picture at a softball tournament in 1984 as part of the Day in the Life of Canada project.

Photo: **Tedd Church**

Jean Frédéric Tremblay of Collège André Grasset comes in for a rough landing after an unsuccessful pass play during a game at John Abbott College.

Photo: **John Mahoney**

The look of sheer ecstasy on the face of Canadian sprinting star Donovan Bailey made this one of the most memorable moments of the 1996 Atlanta Olympics. Bailey set a world record of 9.84 seconds for the 100 metres.

Photo: **Bernard Brault**

Runners swarm the Jacques Cartier Bridge for the start of the 1982 Montreal Marathon.

Photo: **Bernard Brault**

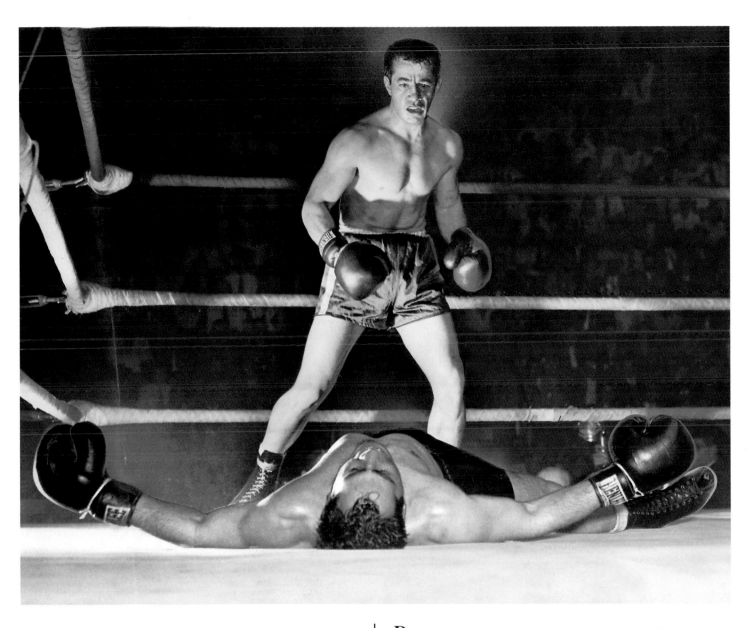

David Bier's famous mat-level photo of Rocky Graziano after he floored opponent Johnny Greco won a National Newspaper Award for best spot news photo for 1951. It is particularly striking in its composition and lighting. Bier, who worked for the Montreal Star, the Montreal Herald and The Gazette, set the standard for newspaper photography in Montreal in the 1940s and 1950s. This photo was shot for the Herald, the archives of which have been merged with those of The Gazette.

Photo: **David Bier**

The passion of the game is caught in the faces of a manager and umpire arguing over a close call at first base.

Photo: **Dave Sidaway**

Violence is a big part of professional hockey but it's rare that referees are on the receiving end of punches like the one captured in this January 1995 photo. Linesman Gerard Gauthier is slugged by Mike Peluso of the New Jersey Devils when his fist, intended for Lyle Odelein of the Canadiens, bounced off Odelein's helmet and caught Gauthier instead. Gauthier needed six stitches.

Photo: **Allen McInnis**

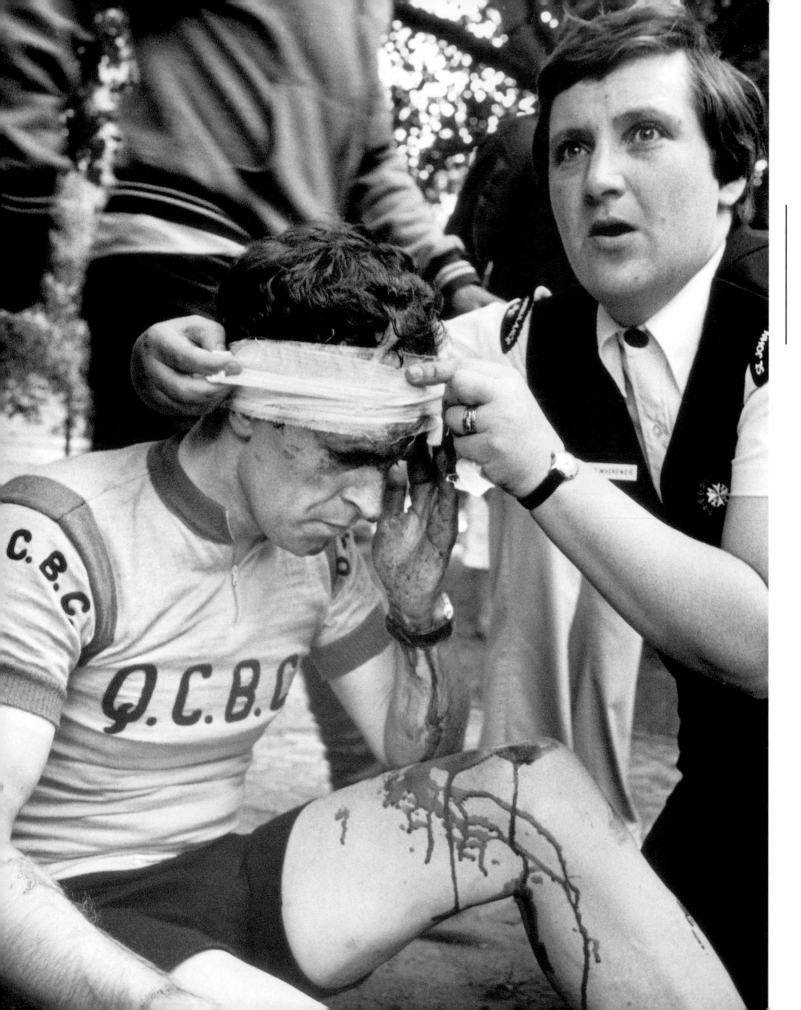

An ambulance attendant cares for a cyclist who took a bad spill after a pile-up in the final minutes of a race at Queen's Park in Toronto.

Photo: **Dave Sidaway**

Wrestler Édouard Carpentier lands a finishing blow in a 1958 match against Wladek (Killer) Kowalski.

Photo: **Michel Gravel**

Gopher it. This furry critter jump-starts at the Montreal Grand Prix in 1989 as Ricardo Patrese's race car roars in the background.

Photo: **Bernard Brault**

They start young in Canada's national sport. These 4- and 5-year-old hockey tykes are waiting for their turn on the ice.

Photo: **Tedd Church**

A runner slides home, too late. Anticipation is key to shooting great sports action shots. When there is a runner on third, all lenses are focused on home plate.

Photo: **Dave Sidaway**

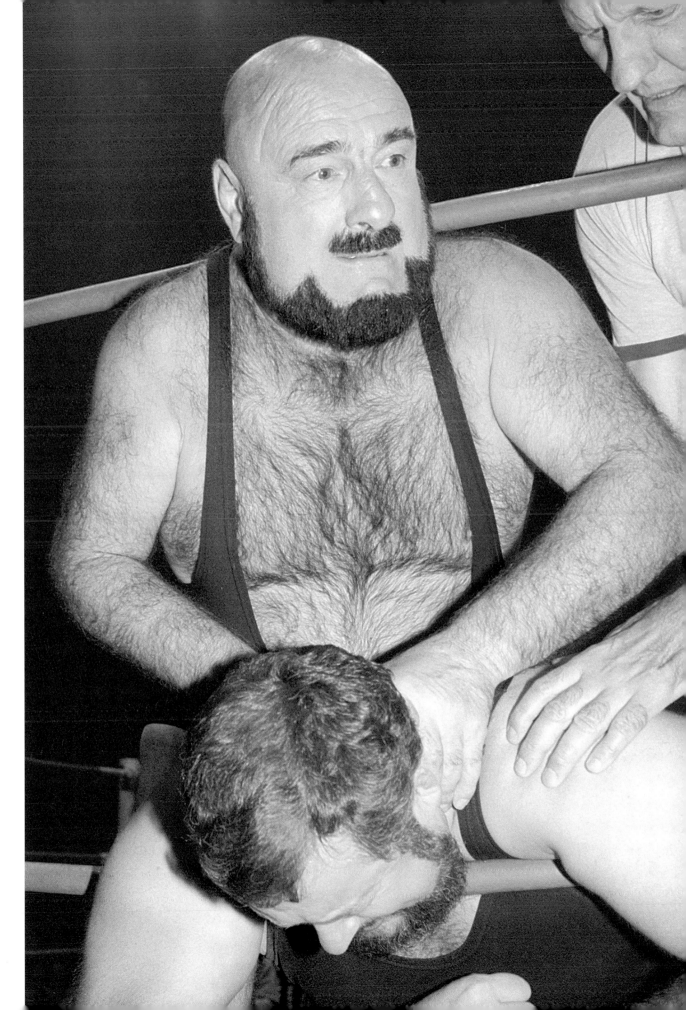

Quebec wrestling superstar Maurice (Mad Dog) Vachon exhibits his fighting form by sitting on the neck of his opponent, Gilles (The Fish) Poisson.

Photo: **Bernard Brault**

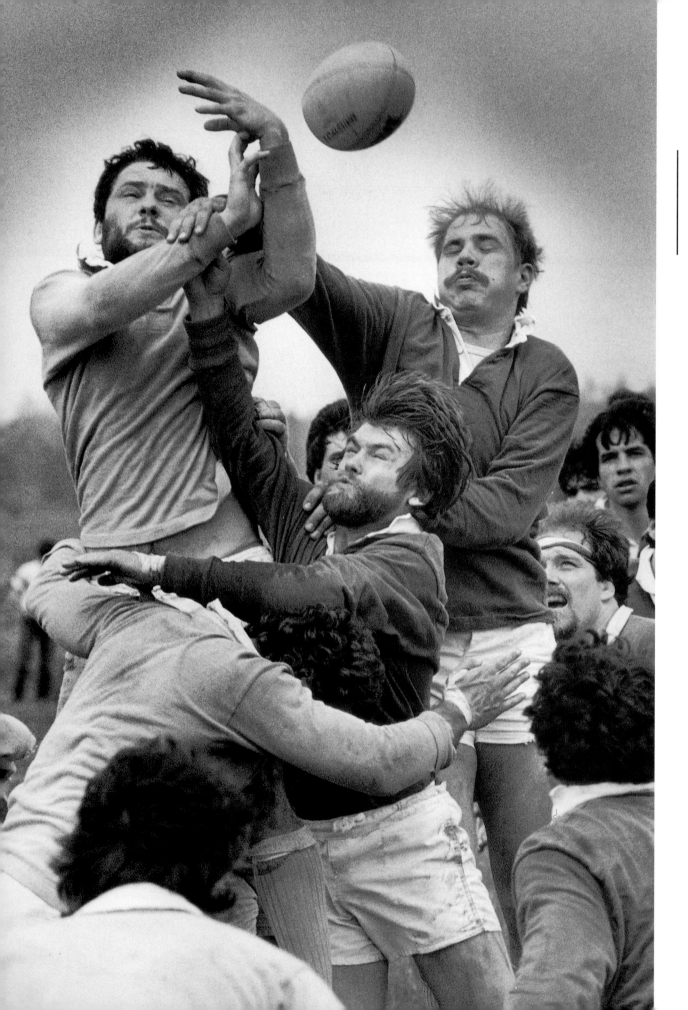

What these rugby players lack in technique, they make up in true grit in this May 1984 clash between the Montreal Irish and a team from Stoney Creek, Ont.

Photo: **George Bird**

He could have been kilt. Or badly hurt. This curler was swept off his feet during a re-enactment of a curling game at the Old Fort on Île Ste. Hélène.

Photo: **Gordon Beck**

Faces

Shooting faces in the news and in the community is one of the most challenging parts of the photographer's job. Getting a photograph that transcends the ordinary and that, at the same time, illustrates the stories and events is never easy. People's expressions tell a big part of the story. Sometimes, there is a single shot that catches a political figure in an unguarded moment. More often, it is the eye and intuition of the photographer that result in a photo that captures the right mood and expression.

There's no more to this cow than meets the photographer's eye. The cow's head was about to be put up as a decoration in the Western Canadian Pavilion at Expo 67.

Photo: **Tedd Church**

This child staring out a broken window puts a human face on poverty in Montreal.

Photo: **Aussie Whiting**

Competitors at the Canadian Baton Twirling championships in July 1990 show their anticipation and excitement as they wait for the score.

Photo: **Allen McInnis**

The wary look on this woman's face says it all. She was not amused when she found herself caught in the wrong place at the wrong time in January 1999 as the Montreal police riot squad prepared for action against demonstrators on René Lévesque Blvd.

Photo: **Bernard Brault**

Sometimes, things are not what they seem. While this 1991 photograph appears dramatic, in fact, the drama occurred two years earlier when the ship sank in Chandler harbour. The man in the photo who appears to be pulling the doomed ship or escaping a drama at sea is in fact a guide explaining how the ship ran aground.

Photo: **Marie-France Coallier**

Dave Sidaway transcended the mundane mug shot with his photo of U.S. President Ronald Reagan at a G7 meeting in Toronto in 1988. Reagan appeared to be napping while Canadian Prime Minister Brian Mulroney made his presentation. "Everyone knew Reagan could nod off during long-winded speeches, and Mulroney was obliging, so I just kept my eye on Reagan," Sidaway says.

Photo: **Dave Sidaway**

One of the most expressive faces in Canadian politics belonged to Quebec Premier René Lévesque, a delight for newspaper photographers to shoot. "Lévesque was one of those politicians who would always do something for photographers," says Church. "Some of these guys will do anything for a good picture."

Photo: **Tedd Church**

One of the lasting legacies of Quebec Premier Robert Bourassa is the James Bay hydro power development, including the huge LG-2 dam shown here.

Photo: **Jean Goupil**

Parti Québécois cabinet minister Claude Charron reacts to his party's loss in a by-election in the late 1970s.

Photo: **John Mahoney**

The bitter disappointment felt by Quebec Premier
Jacques Parizeau at losing the 1995 referendum on
Quebec independence, by a tiny margin, is captured
in this photo taken during his speech on referendum
night, Oct. 30, 1995.

Photo: **Gordon Beck**

An adoring Parti Québécois delegate kissing Premier Lucien Bouchard's hand captured the sentiment of a party meeting in Montreal in May 2000 that gave him a resounding vote of confidence.

Photo: **André Pichette**

The hovering cat hot-air balloon seems ready to pounce hungrily on this woman on a balcony. In fact, it did. The balloon, participating in the Festival des Montgolfières de Saint-Jean-sur-Richelieu in 1993, made an emergency landing in her back yard.

Photo: **Bernard Brault**

To illustrate a story on Montreal transvestites, Gordon Beck used his artistic eye to compose this striking photo in a club in east-end Montreal.

Photo: **Gordon Beck**

Mother Teresa was a small woman but in this photo, she looms large. John Mahoney captured the stature and presence of this great woman at a press conference at Mirabel airport.

Photo: **John Mahoney**

Snow joke for motorists. The painting behind Rokos Christos expresses how many Montrealers feel about winter storms. Pierre Obendrauf first spotted this mural in a Bleury St. parking lot during the summer and knew that one blustery day, he would return.

Photo: **Pierre Obendrauf**

It's hard to tell where the beard ends and the dog begins in this shot of Santa at the SPCA's Christmas party.

Photo: **Gordon Beck**

The colours of the season frame the faces of these three playful children laughing in fallen leaves.

Photo: **Marie-France Coallier**

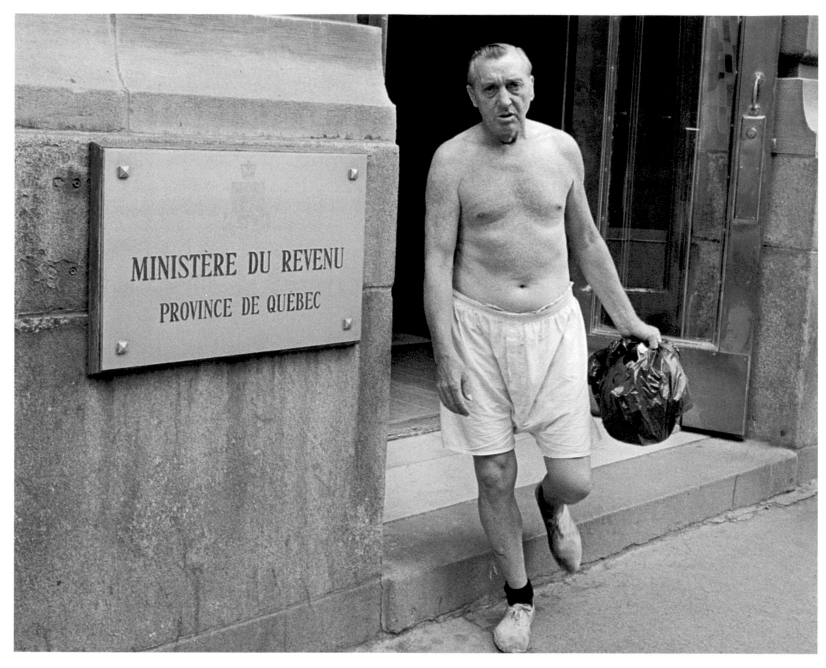

There's an old saying that the taxman will take the shirt right off your back if he can. Michel Gravel captured this taxpayer coming out of the Quebec Revenue Department in July 1970. But no, he didn't lose his shirt. He didn't have it on when he went in. Gravel had been tipped off by a friend who worked at the department that an angry taxpayer was there trying to make a point. Quebecers are the most heavily taxed people in North America.

Photo: **Michel Gravel**

Never without a bottle opener, as long as his teeth hold out. Ward Dickson was mayor of Entry Island, one of the English communities in the Magdalen Islands, when this photo was taken in 1990. At the time, Mayor Dickson also owned the only bar on the island.

Photo: **Peter Martin**

A Mira guide dog named Papineau licks his chops at the sight of his birthday cake as his mistress explains that he must first blow out the candle.

Photo: **Marie-France Coallier**

Ears to you, Mr. Heffner. Michel Gravel caught this amusing shot of Hugh Heffner, the publisher of Playboy, at a news conference in Montreal in July 1967 to inaugurate a nightclub that has since closed. The ears actually belong to a woman sitting beside him, but they are as fetching on him as on any bunny.

Photo: **Michel Gravel**

For many French Quebecers, singer Félix Leclerc and hockey great Maurice Richard are heroes who inspired pride in their home and culture. This photo was taken in 1984 at Leclerc's home on Île d'Orléans as part of a special series in La Presse marking its 100th year.

Photo: **Pierre McCann**

Lamb chopper? This scene caught Bernard Brault's eye while he was visiting Morocco in 1998. With horns honking, a soldier gives a ride to his sheep and his friend.

Photo: **Bernard Brault**

Budding artist Anik Laframboise, 5, puts the finishing touches on a portrait of her mother, Suzanne Drouin, who is trying to get a peek at her daughter's masterpiece. The gift of a good photographer is the ability to capture an ordinary scene like this in a way that conveys the warmth and humour of the moment.

Photo: **John Kenney**

Louise Gagnon is a dog's best friend. Gagnon runs the Miaouf animal shelter in Saint-Simon and was being inundated with appreciation by her canine boarders when this photo was taken in 1996.

Photo: **Pierre McCann**

Eight-month-old Trystan Campbell gets a big
lick out of his meeting with Sorin, a cavalier King
Charles spaniel, at the Montreal International
Dog Show at Place Bonaventure in 1997.

Photo: **John Kenney**

Everybody and his dog was out enjoying the fresh snow at Beaver Lake in January 1995. John Kenney ventured into the middle of a busy toboggan run to take a picture of (front to back) Marcel Lauzon, Rosie and Patrick Amiote. Kenney had been assigned to get a weather picture and the result was this delightful composition.

Photo: **John Kenney**

Hunger and despair are etched on the faces of this Ethiopian mother and her child, photographed during a famine in the 1980s. They were among thousands who had traveled to an aid camp looking for food and help. Aid workers encircled the camp with barbed wire to protect the food stocks.

Photo: **Dave Sidaway**

The mean streets of Montreal are exposed in this disturbing portrait of a woman who spent much of her life in rags and isolation. The photo was taken on St. Laurent Blvd. at a factory that makes cemetery monuments.

Photo: **Tedd Church**

Like father, like son. The son of former Canadiens goalie Patrick Roy shows off his stuff, eager to follow in the tracks of his superstar dad.

Photo: **Bernard Brault**

A young punk and her rat near the corner of Ste. Catherine St. and the Main convey a stark picture of urban life.

Photo: **Gordon Beck**

Back to basics. This couple from Davis Inlet were among those who participated in a retreat in the woods to discuss solutions to the community's social problems.

Photo: **Gordon Beck**

A young resident of Davis Inlet, bundled up to keep warm, is skeptical about a photographer from the south. Gordon Beck was in Davis Inlet for a report on what the community was doing to reduce its high suicide rate and problems of substance abuse.

Photo: **Gordon Beck**

Living

Newspapers are not only about bad news. They are also about

life in the community they serve and the world around.

The photos in this section are snapshots of our lives – vignettes of everyday

living and the little pleasures that are frozen in time,

mirroring our lives and the society in which we live.

A construction worker gets into the spirit of Montreal's annual Jazz Festival, pretending to play his level as a flute.

Photo: **Gordon Beck**

Pierre Lalumière was looking for a feature shot in the summer of 1997 when he spotted these girls, getting into the swing of things, in Lafontaine Park.

Photo: **Pierre Lalumière**

Puppy love.
Photo: **Marie-France Coallier**

Jean-Pierre Reimer, camp monitor at Baldwin Park, is swarmed by young swimmers trying to keep cool on a hot summer's day in August 1996 when the temperature climbed to 30 degrees Celsius.

Photo: **Robert Skinner**

Four youngsters take the plunge on a beautiful summer evening in June 1999 off the wharf at Berthier-sur-Mer, 50 kilometres east of Quebec City.

Photo: **Bernard Brault**

"**M**on pays, ce n'est pas un pays, c'est l'hiver." The words of Quebec folk singer Gilles Vigneault are often proven true in Montreal. This scene of commuters making the home run on a snow-clogged highway during afternoon rush hour is all too familiar.

Photo: **Michel Gravel**

The show must go on. A Montreal musician scales the snowy steps of Place des Arts with his double bass hoisted on one shoulder.

Photo: **John Kenney**

An elderly couple take a twilight stroll down a path through the woods in Stanley Park in Vancouver. The shadows and composition capture the serenity of the moment.

Photo: **Gordon Beck**

Even an ordinary scene in a park can be turned into a work of art with the right photographic eye. The subject and composition are what make this photo of a group of men playing checkers in Lafontaine Park so superb. This simple scene is a whole story in itself.

Photo: **Pierre McCann**

Irish thighs were flashing as this band member lifted his kilt to impress a photographer at the annual St. Patrick's Day parade in Montreal in March 1999.

Photo: **André Pichette**

Two squeegee kids, wiped out
after a day of washing windshields,
relax on the Main.

Photo: **Allen McInnis**

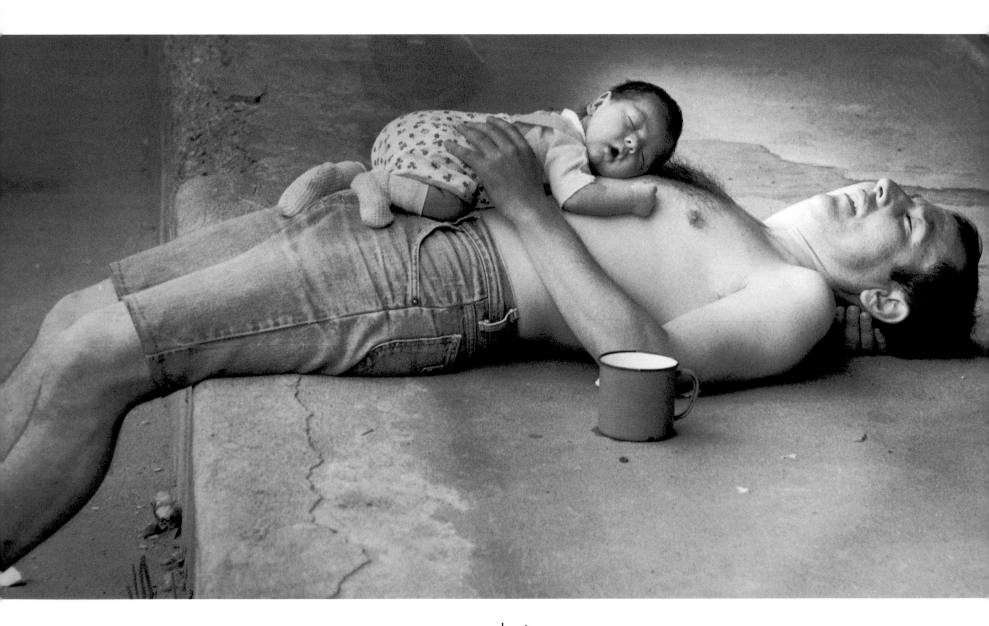

A man and his baby take time out for a siesta on a cement wall in downtown Montreal on a hot summer's afternoon.

Photo: **Tedd Church**

A trainer provides a helping hand to an elephant as circus workers pack up after a show at the Montreal Forum.

Photo: **Tedd Church**

Beauty is in the eye of the beholder. Gordon Beck photographed this man wearing chaps and displaying his bottom at Montreal's Gay Pride parade in 1994.

Photo: **Gordon Beck**

Montreal policeman Michel Primeau helps a group of penguins file across Ste. Catherine St. at St. Urbain in downtown Montreal. The penguins had just left a press conference announcing a Santa Claus parade and were on their way to change when Pierre Obendrauf spotted them.

Photo: **Pierre Obendrauf**

This girl's pose in front of a mural makes you wonder which side is up.

Photo: **Michel Gravel**

Workers pouring hot tar onto a roof on a hot summer day under the spires of Ste. Cunégonde Roman Catholic church on St. Jacques St. caught the artistic eye of Tedd Church. In silhouette, he said, they almost looked as if they were dancing.

Photo: **Tedd Church**

Veteran diver and photographer Pierre Obendrauf captured the eerie atmosphere at the bottom of Lake Ontario with this photo of diver Ingo Eckstein examining the ghostly remains of the wreck of the Sheboygan.

Photo: **Pierre Obendrauf**

Some like it hot. Others, however, like Frédérick Grenier and Pierre Langevin, prefer to cool off from the 32-degree-Celsius heat in the fountain at the Museum of Contemporary Art.

Photo: **Robert Skinner**

Like a throwback to Dickensian London, a chimney sweep is hard at work on a roof in Laval's Ste. Dorothée district. Tedd Church was on his way to a fashion shoot north of Montreal when he spotted this chimney sweep decked out in top hat and tails.

Photo: **Tedd Church**

A man enjoys a moment of solitude in the shade of a tree during a heat wave.

Photo: **Marcos Townsend**

Just happy to be together, Alex Olivier, 2,
of St. Laurent and his dad, Robin,
celebrate spring on Île Ste. Hélène.

Photo: **Gordon Beck**

A group of Brownies and their leader troop home after watching a performance of the RCMP Musical Ride on Île Ste. Hélène to celebrate the 85th anniversary of the Girl Guides of Canada in September 1995.

Photo: **John Kenney**

Photographers

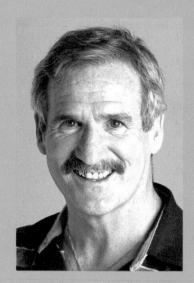

Richard Arless Jr.
The Gazette

Gordon Beck
The Gazette

David Bier
The Gazette

George Bird
The Gazette

Bernard Brault
La Presse

Phil Carpenter
The Gazette

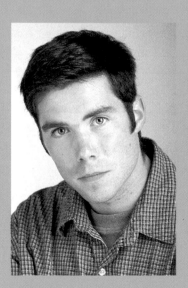

Martin Chamberland
La Presse

Tedd Church
The Gazette

Marie-France Coallier
The Gazette

Pierre Côté
La Presse

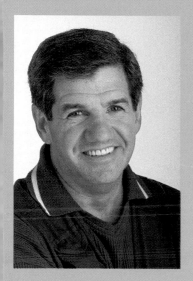

Denis Courville
La Presse

Jean Goupil
La Presse

Michel Gravel
La Presse

John Kenney
The Gazette

Pierre Lalumière
La Presse

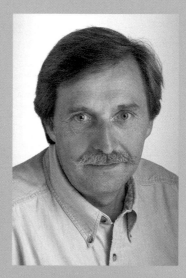

John Mahoney
The Gazette

Robert Mailloux
La Presse

Peter Martin
The Gazette

Pierre McCann
La Presse

Allen McInnis
The Gazette

Robert Nadon
La Presse

Pierre Obendrauf
The Gazette

André Pichette
The Gazette

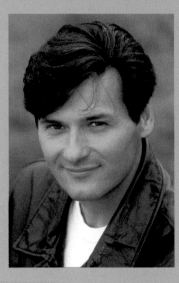

Dave Sidaway
The Gazette

Robert Skinner
La Presse

Roger St-Jean
La Presse

Paul-Henri Talbot
La Presse

Marcos Townsend
The Gazette

Armand Trottier
La Presse

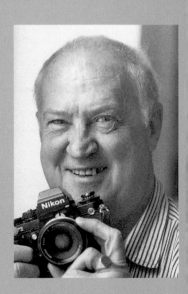

Aussie Whiting
The Gazette